Fa la la la la La la la la

Level 2

Christmas Piano Favorites

Arranged by Mark Sarnecki

Fa la la la la la la la la © 2023 by San Marco Publications. All rights reserved.

All right reserved. No part of this book may be reproduced in any form or by electronic or mechanical means including Information storage and retrieval systems without permission in writing from the author.

ISNB: 9781896499352

CONTENTS

Angels We Have Heard On High	4
Away In A Manger	12
Deck The Halls	8
The First Noel	16
Huron Carol	14
Jingle Bells	6
O Christmas Tree	20
Silent Night	10
We Wish You a Merry Christmas	18
What Child is This?	22

Angels We Have Heard on High

Traditional

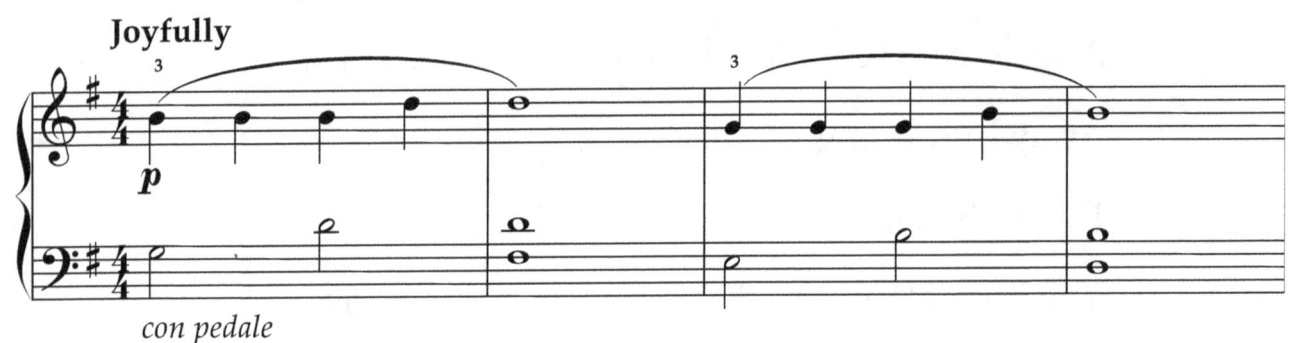

Jingle Bells

Traditional

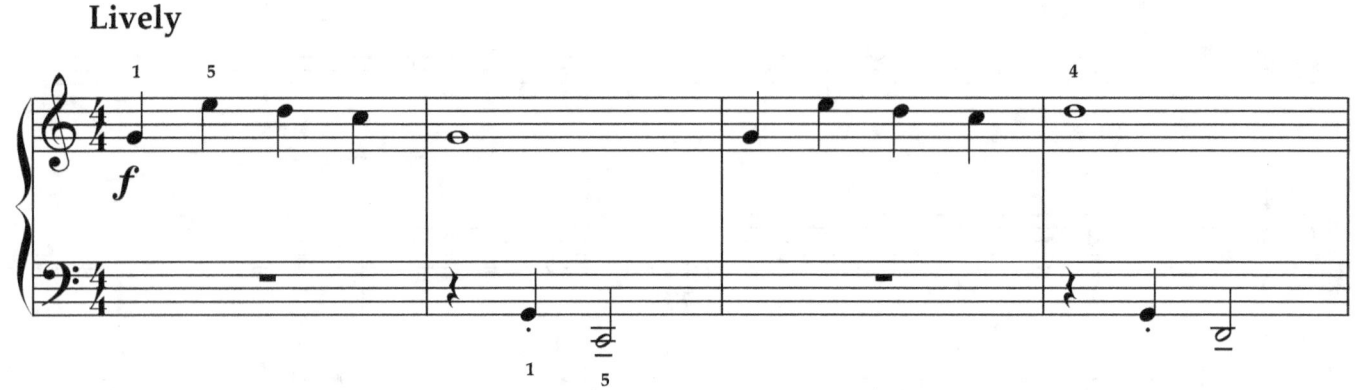

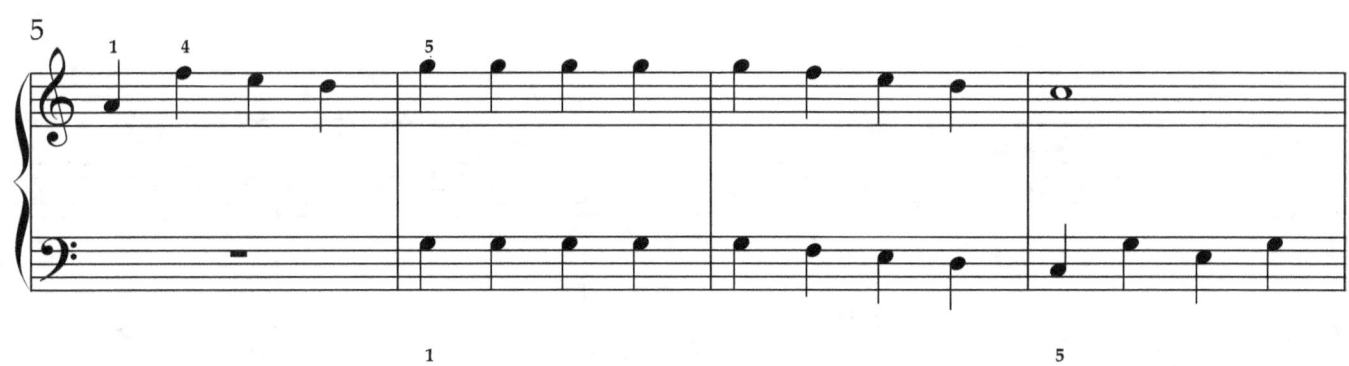

Deck the Halls

Traditional

Merrily

Silent Night

Franz Gruber

Away in a Manger

Traditional

Huron Carol

Traditional

We Wish You a Merry Christmas

Traditional

O Christmas Tree

Traditional German Carol

Slow and Expressive

con pedale

What Child is This?

English Traditional

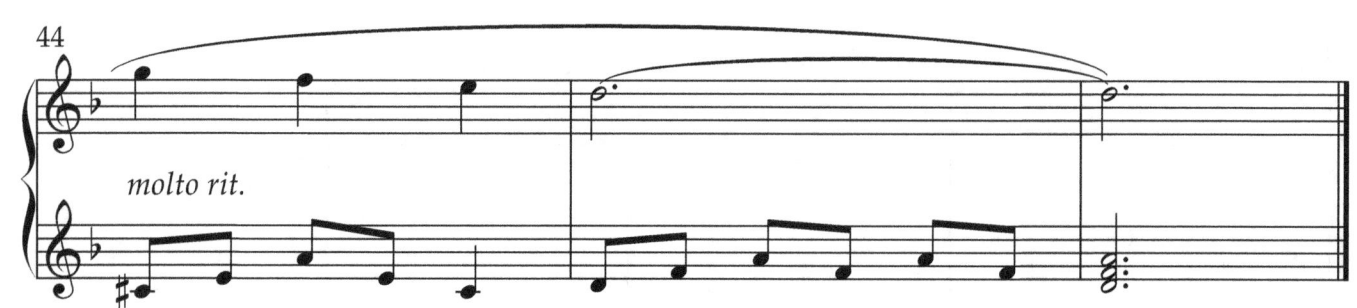